OPERATION IMAGINATION

WITH BUDDY THE BEAR

"Gone Fishing"

Written

By

Joshua Horton

Illustrated

By

Julie De Abreu

To Ethan, Elliot, Eliana, and
to all children who choose to gaze at the stars
rather than always be entertained with a screen.

Before you begin:

There is a good story in this book, I promise. Still, I am quite sure that you can make it a great story. The pictures are not in color, because I believe that YOU can color them much better than I ever could. You will also be able to write your own thoughts and draw your own pictures to add to the story of Buddy the bear and his forest friends. Whatever you do when you read this book, I hope you have fun with it, and most importantly, use your imagination!

Buddy opened his eyes to a warm, sunny day. As he got out of his bed and walked over to a window, he could see the sunlight shining through it. Buddy thought,

Oh, what a nice day. This day is a gift for everyone to enjoy! He also thought about all the beautiful things in the world.

What is something beautiful to you?
Maybe a snow covered mountain, a sunrise,
or a pretty bird?

Just then, someone knocked on his front door. I wonder who that could be, Buddy thought. When he opened the door, he was so surprised to see his best friend, Travis the Turtle!

"Travis! I'm glad to see you."

"Are you ready Buddy?"

"Ready for what?"

"For the Fantastically Fun Friday Fishing Festival!"

Can you say what Travis <--- said five times fast?

Travis may have been slower at walking than most animals, but he could sure talk fast.

"Oh that's right Travis! I almost forgot! Just let me make my bed."

While Travis waited, he talked all about the big day.

"Everyone is going to be there! Becky Beaver, Matty Mouse, Roy Rabbit and..."

"I'm all set and ready to go!" Buddy said with excitement.

Do you know what excitement means. It's when you get really happy about something. What makes you excited or happy?

With a curious look, Travis asked, "How did you make your bed so quickly? That was fast!"

Buddy smiled. "Um, I sleep on a stone with a blanket. It's not that hard to do."

For just a few seconds, Travis and Buddy looked at each other in silence, but it wasn't long until they burst into laughter.

What is something really funny to you?

Who makes you laugh the most?

Buddy sleeps on a stone bed with a blanket.

Try to draw in the box below what you think his bed looks like.

As they headed to the festival, Buddy tried
not to be in a hurry, because he knew Travis
would have a hard time keeping up.

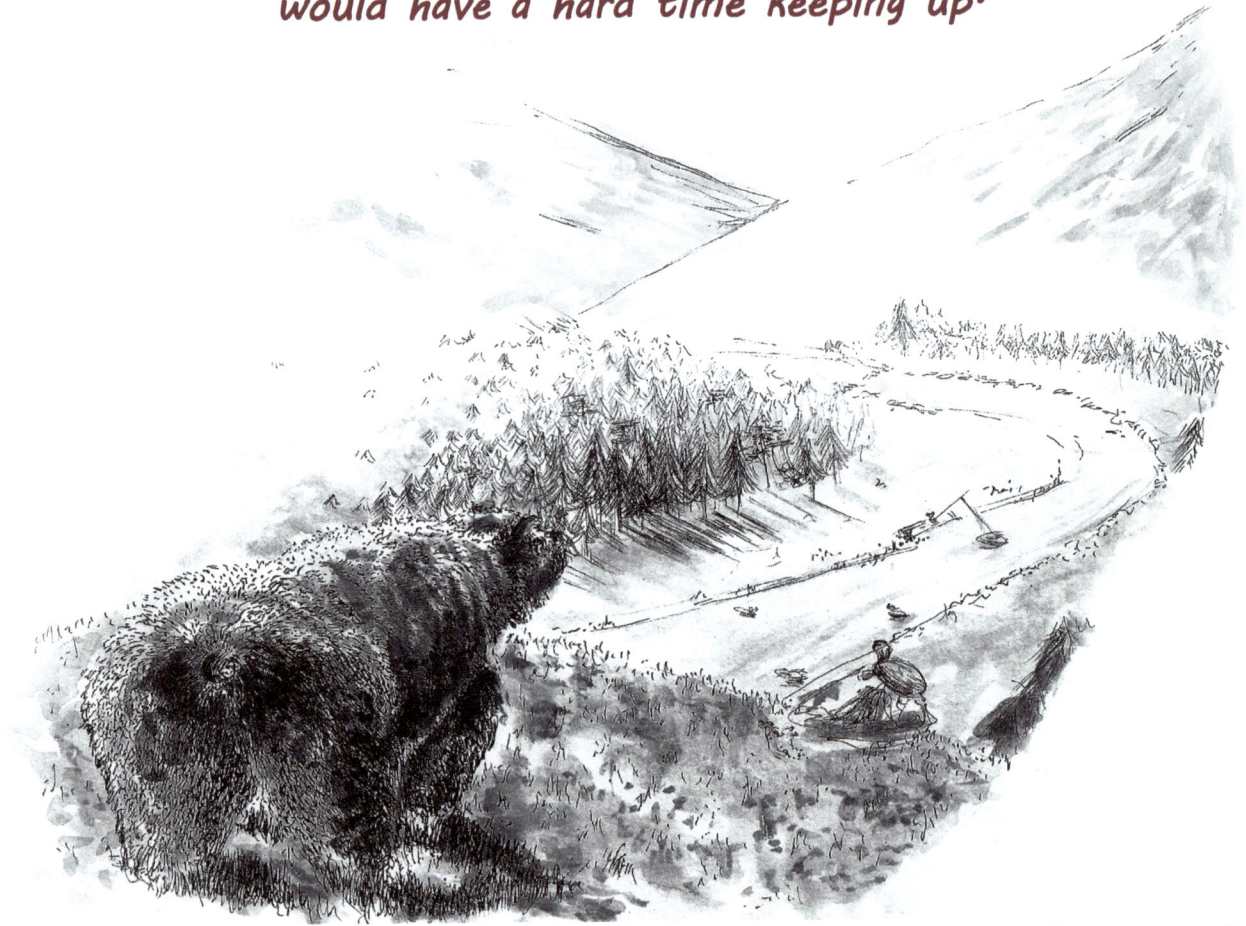

Finally they arrived. As they crossed over a hill,
they could see everyone from Fantastic Forest.

There were so many animals at the festival, but Buddy was particularly surprised to see Sammy Sloth.

Usually Sammy does not leave his home from the top of the trees, unless he is very, very hungry. Of course, at the moment, Sammy was gobbling down several pies even before the pie eating contest.

Buddy had a hard time deciding what to do first at the festival, because there were so many things to choose from. He could swing on the vines, play pine cone toss, participate in a pie eating contest (this was his favorite), and fish in Respite River.

He even saw Roy Rabbit and Argus Alligator having a rock skipping competition.

Buddy would love to know what fun activity you like to do. Let him know by writing down what it is and why you like it so much.

_____

_____

_____

_____

_____

As Buddy made his way over to the pie stand, he heard someone shout near the river. "Help! I've got a big one!" He ran and saw that it was Matty Mouse. He was holding on tight to his fishing pole, but was about to fall into the river!

Buddy quickly grabbed Matty with his big paws, but found out that he was going to need a lot more help to pull out whatever was on Matty's fishing line.

"Come on everyone, we need your help, please!" Buddy shouted.

One by one, all the animals came to help, well almost; Sammy Sloth was too busy eating the rest of the pies to hear all the commotion.

Buddy's favorite food is baked fish dipped in honey!
What is your favorite food?

With one mighty tug from all the animals helping,
Matty made his first catch of the day!

But wait...what's this? It wasn't a fish at all.
On the ground in front of everyone was a wooden chest!

Buddy smiled and said, "Gee Matty, umm...you sure have a strong fishing pole. I think you won this years Biggest Catch Contest." Matty happily told all who helped, "Let's just say we all won this year."

What do you think is inside the chest? Treasure? Dirty socks? It could be anything! Draw in the box what you think it is.

Soon Sammy noticed all the commotion and walked to where everyone was at. Immediately Sammy shouted, "Wow. That's a nice box! It's mine. I found it!"

More than eating lots of food, Sammy liked getting new stuff and even though his stomach was full of pies, somehow he still ran to the chest and tried to open it with all his might while shouting, "I wonder what's inside!"

Everyone tried to warn Sammy that he was pushing the chest back in the water, but he would not listen. He could not get the box open, so he got very mad and started jumping on the lid.

No one had ever seen Sammy move so much, but being greedy and getting mad can make you do crazy things.

Soon Sammy began to wonder why he was getting shorter or maybe everyone was getting taller.

He didn't understand that the chest was sinking, until he felt water under his paws. "Wait, whoa! Help me please!" Sammy shouted.

Why do you think Sammy didn't notice that he was sinking on the wooden chest?

Buddy was a good swimmer and quickly rescued Sammy from the river.

Argus Alligator and Travis Turtle tried to find the wooden chest for Matty, but it was no use. It must have gotten carried away by the river, before sinking all the way down.

As Matty began to walk sadly back to his house, Buddy picked him up by his paw and said, "Matty, you may have lost whatever was in that box, but you will always have your friends."

Matty smiled and gave Buddy a big hug.
Well, as big of a hug that a mouse can give.

The End

Or...

How do you think this story should end?
Would you end it with Matty getting the treasure chest
back or maybe by Sammy giving Matty a gift to apologize?
Write down how you would end the story.

_____

_____

_____

_____

_____

_____

_____

www.ingramcontent.com/pod-product-compliance
Lightning Source LLC
Chambersburg PA
CBHW040024050426

42452CB00002B/121